COACHING
OUR FAMILY BUSINESS

Devotions for Coaches and Spouses

ROGER LIPE

COACHING: OUR FAMILY BUSINESS

Cross Training Publishing
www.crosstrainingpublishing.com
(308) 293-3891
Copyright © 2019 by Roger D. Lipe
ISBN: 978-1-938254-99-4

Unless otherwise noted, all Scriptures are from the Holy Bible, New Living Translation, copyright © 1996, 2004, 2015 by Tyndale House Foundation. Used by permission of Tyndale House Publishers Inc., Carol Stream, Illinois 60188. All rights reserved.

The Love Languages section references the Five Love Languages as described in *The 5 Love Languages: The Secret to Love that Lasts* by Gary Chapman.
Publisher: Northfield Publishing; Reprint edition (January 1, 2015) ISBN-10: 9780802412706

Back cover photo credit: Byron Hetzler

Introduction

A number of years ago I asked Chris Lennon, wife of then Southern Illinois University Football Head Coach Dale Lennon, to speak at a Fellowship of Christian Athletes Coaches and Spouses Appreciation Dinner. Among her insightful remarks was the line, "We decided to make coaching our family business." I thought that was brilliant and portrayed very well a tremendous approach to the consuming lifestyle of coaching. Since then I have referenced Chris' comments with many coaches and their spouses. I am very thankful to have known this great coaching family.

This book contains two series of devotional thoughts specifically written for coaches and their spouses. The first is based on *The 5 Love Languages* as detailed in the excellent book by Gary Chapman. The second set builds on the seasonal nature of sport and the seasonal nature of coaching family lives.

We understand the very busy nature of your lives, therefore the thoughts are brief and direct. They are designed so you may read them separately or together as a couple. There are questions at the end of each day's reading for private contemplation or discussion.

Thanks to the following people who contributed to this project: my wife of forty-four years, Sharon, to Jenn Lipe for editing, and my mentor Fred Bishop for inspiration. Thanks to Don Padgett, and to Bill and Linda McElroy for their hospitality and the solitude of their cabins.

Coaching: Our Family Business

Section 1 – Love Languages*

Words of Affirmation
- Gracious Words - Pure Heart
- Bless, Praise, and Affirm
- Speak Peace and Courage.
- You are Beautiful in Every Way
- Handsome Beyond Words

Quality Time
- At Rest, At Peace, Renewed
- At Dinner with Jesus
- Quiet Rest
- Come Away, My Love
- I've Been Very Eager For This Meal

Acts of Service
- The Leaders Serve
- The Greatest Serve Everyone
- The Godly Serve Sacrificially
- Extravagant, Loving Service
- Do As I Have Done

Giving and Receiving Gifts
- Gifts Open Doors
- Gifts Soothe Angry Hearts
- Jesus Gives Gifts
- Lavish Gifts
- A Gift Too Wonderful for Words

Physical Touch
- He Touched Me
- Who Touched Me?
- One Healing Touch
- Sweet Lips
- My Lover's Embrace

Gracious Words – Pure Heart

Words of Affirmation
Day 1
Proverbs 22:11

Gracious words come from a pure heart. When our hearts are pure, our speech is seasoned with grace, and we find favor with our spouse, with our friends and colleagues, and even with the powerful and influential. We have all seen the results of speech that's less than gracious, speech that betrays a less than pure heart. We might be careful to speak graciously to those in authority, or even to our colleagues, but sometimes our spouses receive the bitterness of our day's frustrations in our unguarded expressions.

King Solomon of Israel wrote eloquently about the kind of speech that reveals hearts and finds favor with people. In Proverbs chapter 22 and verse 11 we read, "Whoever loves a pure heart and gracious speech will have the king as his friend." Solomon was the king, and he knew exactly how words of affirmation and gracious speech won his favor. He chose friends whose gracious speech revealed their love for pure hearts.

In our coaching families, we would do well to take a lesson from King Solomon. We can discern the hearts of those we love by the nature of their words. Listen for the hints of pain, frustration, confusion or fear. Listen for the subtle expressions of respect, loyalty, and love.

Gather a circle of friends who love pure hearts and gracious speech. These are the best kinds of friends. Surround yourself, your spouse, and your children with people whose words of affirmation build up and don't tear down. Find colleagues and players who know how to speak to the hearts of the team. Build your coaching family on wise, gracious, loving words of affirmation, and you'll find you have wide favor, maybe even with the king.

Questions for Contemplation and Discussion:

1. If you were to give yourself a letter grade on graciousness of speech at home with your family (A, B, C, D, or F), what grade would you receive? What grade do you think your spouse or children would give you?

2. How would your coaching colleagues or players grade your speech at practice or training?

3. How do you recognize pure hearts in other people?

4. List three ways you can further develop gracious speech.
   - _____
   - _____
   - _____

Bless, Praise, and Affirm
Words of Affirmation
Day 2
Proverbs 31:28-29

Very few things touch a woman's heart so deeply as when she hears words of affirmation from those she loves. The crayon work of art carried home from kindergarten that has the words "I luv you mommy" scrawled above the dinosaurs will surely find a place of prominence on the refrigerator and deeply in mother's soul. A genuine expression of love and respect by a husband for his wife can wipe away hours of exasperation from a young mother, who may also be a coach.

King Solomon included a section of Proverbs 31 about a wife of noble character, and in verses 28 and 29 he shares some words of affirmation such a woman is due. "Her children stand up and bless her. Her husband praises her: 'There are many virtuous and capable women in the world, but you surpass them all.'" Can you see this in your mind? Have you seen it with your eyes?

This woman's children rise to their feet, in a gesture of respect, and they bless her with words of affirmation. Imagine this happening at the dinner table. Can you see this happening on your mom's birthday? What would her children say to bless her?

As she's wiping away the tears from her children's words of affirmation, her husband stands to speak. He says that in a world full of excellent and praiseworthy women, his wife is the absolute best. Can your heart fathom the depth of joy and emotion her soul would experience?

I would challenge you to follow Solomon's lead to bless, praise, and affirm the women in your life. That includes your mother, your mother-in-law, and your bride. Lead your children to do so. As young men express their hearts to their mothers, they are better prepared to be men who speak words of affirmation to their wives. As young women experience this, they see the loving, expressive heart of a man. This is what they will expect from their husbands.

Questions for Contemplation and Discussion:

1. When was the last time your coaching family took a moment to bless, praise, and affirm mom?

2. If you were to bless your spouse with words of affirmation like this husband did, what would you say? Where and when would be the best place and time for such a declaration?

3. Make a list of the traits your wife possesses that make her "surpassingly virtuous and praiseworthy."

- _____
- _____
- _____

Speak Peace and Courage
Words of Affirmation
Day 3
John 16:33

Life in coaching will surely throw you some curve balls, but wisely chosen and timely spoken words can bring peace and courage to the hearts of everyone affected. Coaching families are nomadic. You move often, too often for some, and that disrupts many of the normal rhythms of life. Changes of address, schools, and friends can feel like chaos and produce fear in our hearts.

Jesus was walking through an avalanche of fear, isolation, and impending violence as he spoke with his team in John chapter 16. At verse 33 we read Jesus' words of affirmation to His disciples: "I have told you all this so that you may have peace in me. Here on earth you will have many trials and sorrows. But take heart, because I have overcome the world." Within hours He would be betrayed, tried, scourged, crucified, and buried, yet He speaks of peace and having overcome the world.

Rather than candy coating the gravity of their situation, Jesus spoke directly about the trials and sorrows to come for his team. His aim in speaking clearly was that they would have peace in Him. It was the disciples' relationship with Christ Jesus that would afford them peace in the midst of trial and sorrow.

Jesus went further, telling them to take heart, because He had overcome the world. I imagine this statement was hard for John to understand as he watched Jesus' crucifixion the following morning. Though hard to grasp, it was an enduring truth that carried John through a long life filled with trial and sorrow, as well as joy and significance.

Words of affirmation, like Jesus spoke to His disciples, can be just the prescription our families need to connect with the peace and courage the Lord promises. He has overcome the world. I am sure he can handle the trials and sorrows we experience in coaching. Speak words of affirmation to your coaching family. Your peace is in relationship with Jesus, and He has overcome the world.

Questions for Contemplation and Discussion:

1. What are the most common sources of trial and sorrow for your coaching family?

2. How do you experience Jesus' peace while walking through those tough times?

3. What are some words you can use to speak peace and courage to your family?

You are Beautiful in Every Way.

Words of Affirmation
Day 4
Song of Songs 4:7-9

Words of affirmation, spoken to your spouse's heart, express love, devotion, affection, desire, and intimacy. Coaches talk for a living and sometimes by the end of the work day they have used up all their syllables. This is a tragic loss for the rest of the family as they each and all need to hear your heart through your voice.

The Bible's most expressive book of poetry is the Song of Songs. In its intimate pages are some of the strongest words of affection, paralleling the love of a husband and wife with that of the Lord Jesus and His bride, the Church. In chapter 4 verses 7 through 9, we read,

> "You are altogether beautiful, my darling,
>> beautiful in every way.
> Come with me from Lebanon, my bride,
>> come with me from Lebanon.
> Come down from Mount Amana,
>> from the peaks of Senir and Hermon,
>> where the lions have their dens
>> and leopards live among the hills.
> You have captured my heart,
>> my treasure, my bride.
> You hold it hostage with one glance of your eyes,
>> with a single jewel of your necklace."

Don't get lost in the geography, focus on the words of

13

affirmation for his bride. He says she is beautiful in every way. He calls her to come away with him. He says she has captured his heart and holds it hostage. One glance from her eyes or one jewel in her necklace is enough to take his heart captive. How often do you speak similarly with your spouse?

Imagine the effect of such words whispered in the ear of your beloved. Coaching families are often inundated by busyness, urgency, long hours, and occasional absences. Our spouses need words like these to affirm their worth, their beauty, and their primacy in our hearts.

Whether a coach or the spouse of a coach, your beloved needs to hear loving, heartfelt, words of intimacy and devotion. Find new and creative ways to express your heart to the one you find to be "altogether beautiful in every way."

Questions for Contemplation and Discussion:

1. In what forms does your spouse best receive your words of affirmation?

> a. Written in a card?
> b. Whispered in an ear?
> c. In a phone call?
> d. Expressed face to face?

2. When will you next say, "You are altogether beautiful, my darling, beautiful in every way. Come away with me"? Where will you go?

Handsome Beyond Words
Words of Affirmation
Day 5
Song of Songs 1:16a

When a woman speaks loving, intimate, private words of admiration to her husband, his heart is filled with warmth, passion, and confidence. Nothing touches a man's soul so deeply as when his beloved speaks words of affirmation to him. Coaches are no exception. Raising championship trophies, receiving coach of the year awards, and every other chest inflating expression pales in comparison with the loving words from his wife's heart.

The Song of Songs chronicles the intimate conversation of a man and his bride along with the running commentary of their friends. In chapter 1 and the first part of verse 16 we read this woman's words of affirmation for her husband, "You are so handsome, my love, pleasing beyond words!" Can you imagine how your husband would respond to these words whispered in his ear?

Even though it is not normally the first thing that attracts a woman to a man, it is surely helpful for him to be easy to look at. She finds her man to be, "so handsome." Further he is, "pleasing beyond words." I would imagine that means everything about his appearance is pleasing.

In a coaching family, it's probably good for a wife to find khaki pants and polo shirts attractive. If so, please tell him he looks good. He probably already thinks so, but to hear you say it will speak to his heart.

Most every coach I know wears confidence like a superhero's cape. They each seem to have a titanium ego and an unassailable self-image, but nothing could be further from the truth. When one is allowed to see beyond the cape and under the mask, many are racked by self-doubt, fear, and anxiety. They need the affirming words of their brides to be at their best. Your expressions of admiration, respect, and even, "You are so handsome, my love, pleasing beyond words!" are of immeasurable worth.

Questions for Contemplation and Discussion:
1. What are a few of your husband's most admirable traits? Write them here.

- _____
- _____
- _____

2. When you picture your coaching husband at his best, what does he look like? What's he wearing? Who is with him?

3. Take a moment to consider how you might tell your beloved, "You are so handsome, my love, pleasing beyond words!"

At Rest, At Peace, Renewed
Quality Time
Day 1
Psalm 23:1-3

To the one whose love language is quality time, simply being together produces rest, peace, and renewal. To merely occupy space in the same room with one's spouse may be enough for him or her. To speak, to touch, to do anything is not really needed. The best stuff in life comes from simply spending time with each other.

King David, the author of Psalm 23, wrote about his experience of quality time this way,

"The Lord is my shepherd;
I have all that I need.
He lets me rest in green meadows;
He leads me beside peaceful streams.
He renews my strength;
He guides me along right paths,
Bringing honor to his name."

David expresses profound contentment as he says, "I have all that I need." He experiences such contentment through rest, peace, and renewal, all provided by his shepherd, the Lord. None of this is due to his achievement but simply a byproduct of spending quality time in the Lord's presence.

In our coaching families, some of the most precious moments are found in the seams between flurries of activity. A few days after the season ends. A week of family vacation is invaluable. A few hours together for a date night are richly rewarding. Any of these can be excellent times of rest, peace, and renewal.

Don't miss them. Build such opportunities into your calendar. Guard them like treasures. These investments of quality time pay rich dividends in your family's present experience and in their future.

Questions for Contemplation and Discussion:

1. When do you and your spouse best experience quality time?

2. Is there a favorite place to go for such time? When did you last go there?

3. Take some time now to build some quality time for family into your calendars.

- What could we do this week to get some quality time?
- Where could we go together this month?
- What could we do as a family later in the year?

At Dinner with Jesus

Quality Time
Day 2
John 12:1-3

Take a moment to recall some of the best times you have had with your spouse over dinner. Can you see the restaurant? Can you hear the laughter, smell the aromas, and taste the flavors? Can you feel the love? Imagine what it would be like to have dinner with Jesus and His friends.

John, the beloved disciple, wrote about such a dinner in his gospel in chapter 12 and verses 1 through 3. There we read, "Six days before the Passover celebration began, Jesus arrived in Bethany, the home of Lazarus – the man he had raised from the dead. A dinner was prepared in Jesus' honor. Martha served, and Lazarus was among those who ate with him. Then Mary took a twelve-ounce jar of expensive perfume made from the essence of nard, and she anointed Jesus' feet with it, wiping his feet with her hair. The house was filled with the fragrance."

Jesus was most at ease, most at rest, in the home of Lazarus and his sisters, Martha and Mary. This is where He experienced quality time. On this particular occasion the quality time is exponentially increased by Mary's extravagant expression of love and devotion.

This occurs just a couple of days prior to his betrayal, trial, and death by crucifixion. Mary grasps the significance of the moment and pours out a lavish gift upon her friend, her Savior. The years of quality time spent in this household had prepared the way for this very expensive and powerfully fragrant moment.

Consider the quality time you have with your coaching family. It is invaluable. When you are together, be 100% present. Put away all the distractions. Be as purposeful and extravagant in your expressions of love and devotion as Mary was. Whatever it costs, they are worth every dime.

In every family, time is fleeting. It seems we're changing a child's diapers one day and walking the aisle at their wedding the next. It is even more so among coaching families. Take full advantage of every moment you have. Be like Mary and pour out every drop of love you have in every second of quality time you have with family.

Questions for Contemplation and Discussion:
1. What memories of dinner with your spouse came to mind? When will you do that again?

2. When do you see some possibilities of quality time coming in your schedule?

3. Make a list of the most common distractions to your quality time and talk about how to eliminate them.

- _____
- _____
- _____

Quiet Rest
Quality Time
Day 3
Mark 6:30-32

When are the times you and your spouse need to get away, to have some quiet, to rest? Where do you go to get such quality time? Most coaches I know have a favorite vacation spot, a wooded cabin, a condo near the beach, or a cozy bed and breakfast they frequent.

Jesus and His team also had the need for quality time, for rest, and for renewal. In Mark's gospel, chapter 6 and verses 30 - 32, we read about how Jesus engineered the needed time for his disciples. "The apostles returned to Jesus from their ministry tour and told him all they had done and taught. Then Jesus said, 'Let's go off by ourselves to a quiet place and rest a while.' He said this because there were so many people coming and going that Jesus and his apostles didn't even have time to eat. So they left by boat for a quiet place, where they could be alone."

In my mind this looks like a victorious team returning from a road trip. Their families, the media, and scores of fans have gathered as the bus pulls in. The team just wants to rest, but this excited and noisy crowd is pressing in on them. Like a wise coach, Jesus knows what they need and makes a plan for some quality time alone.

You, coach and spouse, are the ones who lead your family. You can tell when everyone needs to get away from the noise and confusion. You can see the body language in your kids' withdrawn postures. You can read your spouse's annoyed facial expression as that reporter asks another lame question. You can both sense your family's need for some quality time.

May I challenge you to be as quickly responsive as Jesus was? You will be the hero when you echo Jesus' words, "Let's go off by ourselves to a quiet place and rest a while." Regardless of the cost or the inconvenience, when you provide some quality time, even a day or two, it builds trust and loyalty in each one.

Questions for Contemplation and Discussion:

1. Where is your favorite family vacation spot?

2. When was the last time you were there? When will you go again?

3. What is your favorite thing to do on family getaways?

4. Take a moment with your spouse to plan your next family vacation.
- Where shall we go?
- What are our best dates?
- Who is going to make the reservation?

Come Away, My Love.

Quality Time
Day 4
Song of Songs 7:10-12

Where is your favorite romantic getaway? Where do you and your spouse go to hide from the world and to focus on each other? Some of you are probably thinking, "I wish we had such a place." Let's give some thought to what makes for quality time with your spouse.

In chapter 7 of Song of Songs, we read about mature love in full bloom. The poetic words of verses 10 - 12 are rich with images of quality time.

"I am my lover's,
        and he claims me as his own.
Come, my love, let us go out to the fields
        and spend the night among the wildflowers.
Let us get up early and go to the vineyards
        to see if the grapevines have budded,
        if the blossoms have opened.
        and if the pomegranates have bloomed.
There I will give you my love."

This bride finds great joy in simply being claimed by her husband. For her, their relationship is its own reward. He calls her to experience his love in rich, fragrant, delicious, un-hurried hours together.

The quality of their time together is expressed in:
• the beauty of fields dancing in gentle breezes.
• the fragrance of wildflowers in the night air.

- the delicious flavors and lovely sights of a vineyard.
- the beauty and texture of fruit tree blossoms.
- the declaration, 'There I will give you my love.'

Here's the challenge for today. Would you describe your relationship in similar ways? You may not be a poet, but you and your spouse can certainly share a love that is full of beauty, fragrance, delicious tastes, and is pleasant to the touch. For you, like the couple in the poetry, it will be yours if you say, "Come, my love, let's go out. There I will give you my love."

Questions for Contemplation and Discussion:

1. Where is your favorite romantic getaway? When did you first go there?

2. When do you sense that your relationship has become its own reward?

3. When do have these sensory experiences as a couple?
   a. Beauty
   b. Lovely fragrances
   c. Delicious flavors
   d. Pleasant touch
   e. Declarations of love

I Have Been Very Eager for This Meal.

Quality Time
Day 5
Luke 22:14-16

What are some situations that drive you to eagerly anticipate the moment when your soul can connect with your spouse? I would imagine this often occurs near the end of a long, painful, losing season. Maybe it's in the hours after the kids are in bed and you're waiting for your coaching spouse to return from the office or the gym. Imagine Jesus' anticipation prior to His final meal with His disciples, just hours before His life on earth would end.

Luke records the events of the night before Jesus' crucifixion in his gospel. In chapter 22, verses 14 - 16, we read about this last supper: "When the time came, Jesus and the apostles sat down together at the table. Jesus said, 'I have been very eager to eat this Passover meal with you before my suffering begins. For I tell you now that I won't eat this meal again until its meaning is fulfilled in the Kingdom of God.'"

Jesus knows what His disciples do not know. This will be the last Passover they will celebrate together as a team of thirteen men. This moment is crucial to their growth as a team and to the development of each of them as leaders. He knows that He is about to bring the symbolism of the Passover meal into full fruition through His sacrificial death, burial, and resurrection.

Often in the life of a coaching family, one of the spouses can see the approaching events more clearly than the other. Both parents can usually see oncoming trials or challenges long before their children can. This calls for us to be as wise in our anticipation as Jesus was by gathering those we love.

As we become aware of tough times on the horizon, let's be very eager to share with our spouse and our children the gravity of the moment and assure them of God's presence and provision along the way. To gather everyone together, to talk calmly through the anticipated scenario, speaks peace to everyone. For them to experience the loving embrace of quality time strengthens the bonds of love and trust.

Questions for Contemplation and Discussion:

1. In what sorts of situations do you strongly need your spouse to be present?

2. When have you anticipated a tough time ahead and had a helpful talk with your spouse?

3. How can you create quality time with family when you see tough times approaching?

The Leaders Serve
Acts of Service
Day 1
Mark 10:43

How easy or how hard do you find it to serve your spouse? What are the top three household tasks you would rather not do? How much love would your spouse feel if you were to do all three of those chores today? What are the tasks coaches or team leaders perceive to be beneath them? What happens when they do them anyway?

Jesus was a tremendous leader, but He turned the conventional ways of leading upside down. Some of His most direct instructions about how to lead are recorded in Mark's gospel in chapter 10, verse 43. Jesus says this about leaders and service: "But among you it will be different. Whoever wants to be a leader among you must be your servant." After referencing the power-mongering Roman leaders of His day, Jesus makes a sharp contrast for those who would lead in the kingdom of God. He says that leaders serve.

Regardless of your views of proper roles in a family, husbands and wives, fathers and mothers are both leaders. If we are to lead in Jesus' way, it will require us to serve others in the family. Think of it in these terms. What does my spouse need? It is my responsibility to serve that need. It is never my responsibility to demand that my spouse meet my needs. Servants don't make demands.

This posture stands the world's view of leadership on its ear. The best coaches serve their colleagues and their teams.

The best team leaders serve their teammates. At their best, husbands serve the greatest interests of their wives and vice versa. At their best, parents serve the needs of their children. It's about to get even tougher. At their best, couples serve the interests of their in-laws. This is the nature of leadership in Jesus' kingdom. The leaders serve.

Now back to those household chores. I challenge you to ask your spouse about the three that are most distasteful to him or her and then volunteer to take those tasks as your own. This would be Jesus' way to lead and to love.

Questions for Contemplation and Discussion:

1. Have your spouse list his or her 3 least favorite household chores here:

- _____
- _____
- _____

2. Think about some ways that serving is effective leadership in your family.

3. Who has been a good model of leading by serving for you?

4. How can you most effectively lead your family by serving selflessly?

The Greatest Serves Everyone
Acts of Service
Day 2
Mark 10:44

Who wears the pants in your family? Who is the family CEO, the Big Dog, the Numero Uno? If that's you, Jesus would say you must lay down your rights. You didn't see that one coming, did you? It's Jesus' way to flip over the conventional way of doing things.

He does it again in Mark chapter 10, verse 44. Right after telling His disciples to not do things the government way, and saying that those who would be leaders must serve, He continues by saying, "and whoever wants to be first among you must be the slave of everyone else."

This is really backward to the normal way of the world. We usually expect those who are first to have privileges, move to the front of the line, get the best seat, and get first choice. Jesus inverts the whole idea by saying the one who is first must be the slave to everyone else. Slaves have no rights, let alone privileges.

This is Jesus' way, and it is brilliant for leadership of a team or a family. When the greatest among the coaches or players takes the lowest position, he or she lifts everyone else. When the leader of a family forgoes his or her rights and privileges, the whole family is bettered. However, when we tightly clutch our rights, our titles, our status, we push down all those we are pretending to lead.

Okay, Big Dog, here is the challenge. Consider the

rights, privileges, and perks of your position you could relinquish to elevate others. Think about your team, and think about your family. How can you make yourself the slave to everyone else and thereby lead more effectively than ever?

Questions for Contemplation and Discussion:

1. For which family responsibilities do you take the lead and for which does your spouse take the lead? How did you decide those roles?

2. Are you happy with the family leadership roles in which you currently serve? What would you change?

3. What are some perks, rights, or privileges you might need to relinquish to lead more effectively?

The Godly Serve Sacrificially

Acts of Service
Day 3
Mark 10:45

If acts of service are your spouse's love language but not yours, to serve well is sometimes a sacrifice. The good news is that when we serve sacrificially we're acting just like the Lord Jesus. To sacrificially serve our coaching colleagues, our friends, our family, even the random stranger on the street, is the height of Christian leadership.

Jesus completes His trilogy of leadership statements in verse 45 of chapter 10 where we read, "For even the Son of Man came not to be served but to serve others and to give his life as a ransom for many." Let's unfold this pithy sentence, piece by piece, to grasp Jesus' ultimate expression of servant leadership.

First He refers to Himself in third person, the Son of Man. Even the way Jesus speaks is humble, preferring to point to this Messianic title rather than saying, "I." Sacrificial service requires humility.

He asserts that the Son of Man did not come to be served but to serve others. If anyone had the right to be served, we would say it was surely the Son of God, Creator of the universe. Jesus would have none of it. Sacrificial service prefers selflessness.

Jesus goes even further, saying that He was to give His life as a ransom for many. A ransom is the price paid to free another from slavery. It's ironic that the price was normally thirty pieces of silver, exactly the sum Judas received for betraying the Lord. In Jesus' case the ransom was His life. Sacrificial service sets others free.

Coaches and spouses, I challenge you to take up Jesus' way of sacrificial service. Humbly lay down your privilege. Prefer selflessness to guarding your rights. Serve sacrificially and set others free.

Questions for Contemplation and Discussion:

1. What are some acts of service you know your spouse appreciates? How often do you make time to do them?

2. Which of those acts of service are a great sacrifice for you?

3. How does service humble you?

4. What are some privileges you can forgo to serve others better?

5. How has your spouse's service of others freed people to be their best?

Extravagant, Loving Service

Acts of Service
Day 4
John 12:3, 7-8

How does your spouse respond when you serve in a grand, extravagant way, surpassing all expectations? Maybe you washed and detailed the car or you cleaned the dishes, scrubbed the cabinets and mopped the floor. You may have taken the kids and arranged for a day at the spa or called his buddies to join him to watch a game. Oh, you've never done that? Let's watch someone serve extravagantly, and see what happens.

John records a remarkable act of service in his gospel at chapter 12, verse 3, followed by verses 7 and 8. There we read, "Then Mary took a twelve-ounce jar of expensive perfume made from the essence of nard, and she anointed Jesus' feet with it, wiping his feet with her hair. The house was filled with the fragrance. Jesus replied (to Judas), 'Leave her alone. She did this in preparation for my burial. You will always have the poor among you, but you will not always have me.'"

Mary provides an essential service to Jesus: preparation for burial, just days before it is actually needed. She did it extravagantly. This perfume cost a year's wages. She didn't use a towel to wipe His feet, she used her hair! Extravagant, loving service.

Judas criticizes her over-the-top service, calling it wasteful and feigning concern for the poor. Jesus calls him on it and honors Mary's service. He also reframes the discussion by elevating the importance of a moment in Jesus' presence over the mundanity of daily needs.

In leading our coaching families there are always mundane, daily chores and responsibilities. It is always good and proper to fulfill these obligations excellently, but when a moment of significance arises, jump on it with extravagant service. Mary recognized her moment, pounced on it, and we're still smiling about her fragrant service today. Judas missed it entirely, and no one has a fond word to say about him.

My challenge to you is to watch for the divine moment, when you know the Lord Jesus would be pleased with your loving, extravagant, selfless service of another. They're worth it.

Questions for Contemplation and Discussion:

1. What is one act of extravagant service you could provide for your spouse this week?

2. What will it cost to get that done? Is he or she worth it?

3. How will you answer your critics when they say it costs too much?

4. How will you recognize the divine moments when they appear?

5. How do you distinguish such divine moments from more mundane daily tasks?

Do As I Have Done.

Acts of Service
Day 5
John 13:12-15

Who have been the most servant-hearted people in your coaching life? You may have thought about folks from the support staff: trainers, equipment managers, graduate assistants, or video coordinators. They all serve behind the scenes with little fanfare but great loyalty and faithfulness. How well have you followed their examples of selfless service?

John records in chapter 13 the beginning of Jesus' last night with His disciples. Jesus starts by washing the feet of his teammates, and in verses 12 - 15 He explains the significance of this act, "After washing their feet, he put on his robe again and sat down and asked, 'do you understand what I was doing? You call me 'Teacher' and 'Lord,' and you are right, because that's what I am. And since I, your Lord and Teacher, have washed your feet, you ought to wash each other's feet. I have given you an example to follow. Do as I have done to you."

Like most good coaches and teachers, Jesus models for His team what He wants them to do. He disrobes, stoops down, and takes up the lowliest act of service in their culture. He is their Lord and teacher, but He humbly serves them all, even Judas.

Jesus then helps them grasp the significance of His service by instructing them to take His example and to serve each other, even in the most disgusting of tasks.

Let's revisit the earlier thought about servant-hearted

people in your life. Recall their service. Remember their attitudes. Consider the significance of their example. Let's be quick to "wash the feet" of those we lead, in sport and in our family.

Let's watch for the ugly, smelly, lowly tasks, and let's do them with our whole hearts. That will make an indelible impression on everyone who follows.

Questions for Contemplation and Discussion:

1. List three servant-hearted people in your life today:

- _____
- _____
- _____

2. Who are the people in your family who have modeled Christ-honoring service for you?

3. List three tasks others find disgusting that you could take on and thereby model Jesus' way of serving.

- _____
- _____
- _____

Gifts Open Doors
Giving and Receiving Gifts
Day 1
Proverbs 18:16

There are times when presenting a gift will open a door or welcome a valued guest. A well-chosen gift can enhance one's relationship with a spouse. A timely, appropriate gift can bring a coach into the presence of the influential and powerful. How many of these dynamics have you personally experienced? The Bible is full of such expressions of this love language.

One such instance is in Solomon's book of wisdom titled, Proverbs. In chapter 18, verse 16 we read, "Giving a gift can open doors; it gives access to important people." Simply and directly, like most of his proverbs, Solomon states the value of giving gifts. They open doors and they grant us access.

As a coach, you probably give gifts to a wide range of people: family, friends, coaching colleagues, administrators, and others. These gifts open doors, some to offices, and others to hearts and minds. In some cultures there is a very fine line between a gift and a bribe. The same gift, seen either way, will open doors for us.

The wise giving of gifts can also grant us access to the powerful and influential. It's common for a coach to give a pair of tickets to a friend who has the ear of a wealthy donor, a government official, or a prospective employer. That gift may be the key to gaining access to this person's presence, then to his ear, or to gain her favor.

Even beyond the giving of a physical gifts, food, team

gear, or tickets, the gift you give may be your unique set of skills. That may be the gift of greatest value to the important person. Your giftedness may be what opens the door for you. Your abilities may be the very gift most treasured by your next employer, your next recruit, or the financial supporter.

I challenge you to think about the giving of gifts, rather than keys, being the way to open doors and to gain access. Examine your key chain of gifts, abilities, skills, and other assets, and then approach any door you like. You just might have the right stuff.

Questions for Contemplation and Discussion:

1. What are some gifts that have opened doors for you? How did you present them?

2. Whose door would you like to see opened to you? What might be the gift that would open that door and give you access?

3. How important is your spouse to the opening of doors? Could it be that you two are seen as a gift?

Gifts Soothe Angry Hearts

Giving and Receiving Gifts
Day 2
Proverbs 21:14

More than a few husbands have come home from work with a dozen roses in hand, knowing something they have done, or failed to do, had sparked anger. Why do they do that? It's simply because they know that gifts can soothe angry hearts.

Solomon, the King of Israel, knew this as well. He had over 200 wives, and I would imagine he had a standing order for roses at the florist shop. Proverbs chapter 21, verse 14 captures his thoughts on the matter. "A secret gift calms anger; a bribe under the table pacifies fury." I saw your hair stand up when you heard the word "bribe." Hang on for a moment.

Let's start with the secret gift that calms anger. That's the kind one's spouse generally likes: secret, intimate, and private. To give an "I'm sorry" gift in public only throws gasoline on the fire. The gift given in secret soothes the angry heart and helps restore relationship.

In the same vein of thought, a gift given under the table, that is in secret, can put to rest professional contentions. In the world of coaching, the higher the level of sport, the more digits in the salaries, and the more professional the environment, the greater the need is for cool heads and occasional secret gifts to keep the peace. Whether you call them bribes or professional courtesies, they make negotiations go better.

Giving an upgrade on an airline ticket, a suite rather than a more modest hotel room, and car service rather than a taxi, are all ways to give a secret gift that can ease the tension and promote harmony in a working relationship.

Similarly, being a little extravagant for a birthday or anniversary gift, hand writing a card, or spontaneously whisking your spouse away for a weekend can calm some anger and rebuild a relationship beginning to fray at the edges.

When anger and fury raise their heads, counter with a wisely chosen and privately presented gift. It will be cool water poured upon an overheated soul.

Questions for Contemplation and Discussion:

1. When has your spouse come home with an "I'm sorry" gift? Did it have the desired effect?

2. How do you see gifts or even bribes given in your working environment?

3. How might a wisely chosen gift be of benefit to your next tense situation?

Jesus Gives Gifts
Giving and Receiving Gifts
Day 3
Ephesians 4:7-8

What were some of the most special gifts you received as a child? What sorts of gifts do you receive from your spouse and children? Have you also given and received gifts from your coaching colleagues and those you coach? What do the gifts reveal about the givers? We who speak the love language of giving and receiving gifts are simply following the example of the greatest gift giver of all time. Let's take a few pointers from Him.

In the Apostle Paul's letter to his friends in Ephesus, he writes about gifts in chapter 4, verses 7 and 8, "However, he has given each one of a special gift through the generosity of Christ. That is why the Scriptures say,

'When he ascended to the heights,

He led a crowd of captives

And gave gifts to his people."

Paul asserts that the Lord God has given each of us a gift of grace at Jesus' expense. He paraphrases Psalm 68 to affirm his thoughts about God's generosity in Christ.

Let's look at God's gift giving a little closer for further instruction. He gives to each one. He misses no one. He doesn't gift just the most prominent, the most talented, or the loveliest. He gives graciously to each one through the generosity of Christ.

Jesus ascended to the heights, and He has carried a

crowd of captives with him. This is symbolic of the way conquering armies would return to their homeland, bringing the best and brightest of the conquered land with them. We are in Jesus' train of captives, but we are excited and joyously captivated by His love for us.

Paul spins Psalm 68:18 from "You received gifts from the people," to "And gave gifts to his people." The generosity of Christ seems so full of giving that there is no room for thoughts of receiving. Jesus' way of giving never even thinks of what He might receive in return.

Let's all learn to speak the love language of giving and receiving gifts. Let's follow Jesus' example of over-the-top generosity and give lavishly to each one. Let's ascend to the heights of our profession and of coaching family life. Let's lead a crowd of excited and joyously captivated hearts. Let's give with no thought of receiving anything in return. This is Jesus' way.

Questions for Contemplation and Discussion:

1. What were some of those childhood gifts you recalled earlier?

2. What sorts of gifts do you give to others?

3. What do the gifts you have received reveal about the hearts of the givers?

4. How will you follow Jesus' way of giving as described in the final paragraph?

Lavish Gifts
Giving and Receiving Gifts
Day 4
Matthew 2:11

Think about the gifts you received as a child for Christmas or birthdays. Did any of them simply overwhelm you? Have you ever given a gift that would be considered lavish? Imagine your coaching family is rather poor, with graduate assistant parents, and your toddler is suddenly visited by foreign dignitaries who bring priceless gifts. This was the case for Joseph, Mary, and the two-year-old Jesus of Nazareth.

In Matthew's gospel he records the story of the wise men visiting the home of Joseph and Mary to see the child Jesus. In chapter 2, verse 11 we read, "They entered the house and saw the child with his mother, Mary, and they bowed down and worshiped him. Then they opened their treasure chests and gave him gifts of gold, frankincense, and myrrh." Such lavish and extravagant gifts for a two-year-old child, they must see him as an extraordinary person.

Imagine if the head coaches from the greatest sports programs in your region of the world came to visit your toddler with professional contracts and signing bonuses in hand. Imagine Mary's wonder and amazement at the things these men said, the distances they traveled, and the gifts they brought. What does all this mean? Why these gifts? Of all the two year old boys in Israel, why our son? She and Joseph were surely overwhelmed by this spectacle in their modest home in Nazareth.

We hear nothing about the lavish gifts through the rest

of the story; rather the most lavish gift, Jesus Himself, takes center stage for the remainder of Matthew's writing. That simple fact may give us a hint about the true nature of gift giving.

As much as you may labor and fret over purchasing the perfect gifts for loved ones, they are most gratified by the gift of your presence. You are more valuable to them than any trinket or gadget that will begin to diminish in value as soon as it's taken from its box.

Let's learn from the magi and from Mary. The wise men traveled great distances, presented lavish gifts, and marveled at the Christ Child. We would do well to similarly go to great lengths and costs to contribute to others lavishly. Mary received these strangers and stood amazed at their worship. Let's receive strangers hospitably and value the Lord Christ even more than Christmas Day's mountain of gifts.

Questions for Contemplation and Discussion:
1. What was the most lavish gift you have received?

2. To whom have you given lavish gifts? What were they?

3. How would you respond to a knock on the door by gift bearing foreign dignitaries?

4. Whose presence at birthday or holiday celebrations is more valuable to you than any gift they could bring?

A Gift Too Wonderful for Words

Giving and Receiving Gifts
Day 5
II Corinthians 9:13-15

One of the great days in the life of a coaching community is when a highly achieving team receives their championship rings. Broad smiles shine, stories are told, backs are slapped, and everyone from head coach to equipment managers, star players to those who never saw game action, all receive the same ring. The giving and receiving of gifts produces great effects in the lives of all those involved, givers and receivers alike. It even involves and blesses some beyond those most obvious.

The Apostle Paul wrote to his friends in Corinth about the value of giving and receiving gifts. In his second letter at chapter 9, verses 13-15, we read, "As a result of your ministry, they will give glory to God. For your generosity to them and to all believers will prove that you are obedient to the Good News of Christ. And they will pray for you with deep affection because of the overflowing grace God has given to you. Thank God for this gift too wonderful for words." It seems there are gifts being given and received all across this web of relationships.

The church at Corinth, Greece had gathered and sent a gift to the impoverished and persecuted church in Jerusalem, Israel. Their gift was warmly received and resulted in affectionate prayers for the Corinthians, and in giving glory to God.

The Corinthians were eager to contribute to their

friends in Jerusalem because of the gift they had received in coming to Christ Jesus. Their obedience to Christ was honored broadly as they had received the grace of God to give to others.

Paul, the church at Jerusalem, the Church at Corinth, you, and I have all been richly blessed by the gift too wonderful for words: a new life in Christ Jesus. He has purchased our lives by His blood and given us to God the Father in renewed relationship. This is the way of the Kingdom of God, to receive freely and to freely give.

In your coaching family, seek ways to give and receive gifts in similar ways. Lead your children to contribute to the needs of others. Look for ways to make an occasional lavish, way-over-the-top gift. This blesses the giver, the receiver, and the Lord Jesus.

Questions for Contemplation and Discussion:

1. What are some team gifts or awards you have gathered across the years?

2. How valuable are they to you now?

3. When have you experienced more joy in giving gifts than in receiving them?

4. How can you lead your coaching family to be generous in giving to others?

He Touched Me!

Physical Touch
Day 1
Mark 1:40-42

The world of sport is full of physical expression. Handshakes, hugs, slaps on the back, and even pats on the backside are pretty common methods of communication for coaches. How important is touching and being touched to your spouse? Imagine if either of you had a medical condition that forbade anyone to even come near you. Consider how such isolation would suck the very life from you.

Mark's gospel tells the story of a man who was isolated due to leprosy and how he encountered Jesus of Nazareth. In chapter 1, verses 40 - 42, we see how Jesus used physical touch to restore the man. "A man with leprosy came and knelt in front of Jesus, begging to be healed. 'If you are willing, you can heal me and make me clean,' he said. Moved with compassion, Jesus reached out and touched him. 'I am willing,' he said. 'Be healed!' Instantly the leprosy disappeared, and the man was healed."

In that day people with leprosy were forbidden to even be in the room with "clean" people, let alone be in physical contact with them. Jesus defied cultural standards and reached out His hand to touch this diseased man's body. His act of compassion had immediate results.

Coaching families are often in similar situations. Those in need of your healing touch are not usually lepers but are plagued with broken hearts, fractured families, or crushed souls. The sporting community you serve is more like a leper colony than a royal courtyard.

Look beyond the exteriors of muscle, expensive sporting gear, and swagger to see the brokenness of soul that is the daily experience of some among your coaching colleagues, players, and the families of both.

Like the leper in the story, a simple physical touch from you may be a powerful expression of God's healing grace for a leprous heart. Push past your hesitance to get too close, and embrace the injured player. Take the risk to care deeply, and hug the neck of a recently fired colleague. Go beyond your boundaries of comfort and convenience to express the compassion of Christ by simply extending your hand.

Questions for Contemplation and Discussion:

1. How do you use physical touch as a part of how you coach?

2. How important is touching and being touched to your spouse?

3. What are the factors that hold you back from being more expressive with physical touch?

4. What sorts of touch do others in your family find to be expressions of love and care?

Who Touched Me?

Physical Touch
Day 2
Luke 8:43-48

Think for a moment about the largest, thickest, and most chaotic crowds in which you have found yourself. In all that noise, jostling, and confusion, could you still feel your lover's hand in yours? That bond of physical touch is the conduit for a powerful force. In just such a crowd, a similar touch had a dramatic effect upon one person in a crowd with Jesus as He walked through Galilee.

Luke wrote about this miraculous encounter in his gospel in chapter 8, verses 43 - 48. There it says, "A woman in the crowd had suffered for twelve years with constant bleeding, and she could find no cure. Coming up behind Jesus, she touched the fringe of his robe. Immediately the bleeding stopped. 'Who touched me?' Jesus asked. Everyone denied it, and Peter said, 'Master, this whole crowd is pressing up against you.' But Jesus said, 'Someone deliberately touched me, for I felt healing power go out from me.' When the woman realized she could not stay hidden, she began to tremble and fell to her knees in front of him. The whole crowd heard her explain why she touched him and that she had been immediately healed. 'Daughter,' he said to her, 'your faith has made you well. Go in peace."

In the midst of all the pushing and shoving of this crowd, Jesus perceives a particular touch of his robe. Something about this touch was different from all the other bumps and jostles. This touch was one of faith.

This woman and her twelve year affliction were desperate enough to reach out and touch the One she believed could heal her. This is faith: active trust in God. Her trust in Jesus moved her to touch Jesus' robe.

Don't be surprised if those in your family, others among your team and coaching colleagues, and still others in your community reach out to touch you. They can tell there is something different about you. They can't put their finger on it, but they believe you can help. That's what faith looks like. When people are reaching out to you, like this woman reached out to Jesus, perceive their needs as He did, and watch Jesus' healing power restore their lives.

Questions for Contemplation and Discussion:

1. Have you experienced big, chaotic crowds? Do they scare you, or do you enjoy them?

2. When have you been in such a crowd but felt one particular touch from someone?

3. Have you ever been similarly desperate and asked Jesus to do something in your life? What happened?

4. Who has recently reached out to you for help? How did you respond?

One Healing Touch
Physical Touch
Day 3
Luke 13:10-13

If you are like most couples, there are occasionally days or even weeks when things are a little tense between you. For any number of reasons the relationship feels a little tattered and some distance has grown between you. Can you recall the first touch that began the relational healing process? How powerful is a single loving touch to a broken soul? Could it be that one touch would set someone free and restore a broken spirit?

Luke, the gospel writer, was also a medical doctor. He writes in great detail about Jesus' healing of a myriad of people. One such instance is in chapter 13, verses 10 - 13, "One Sabbath day as Jesus was teaching in a synagogue, he saw a woman who had been crippled by an evil spirit. She had been bent double for eighteen years and was unable to stand up straight. When Jesus saw her, he called her over and said, 'Dear woman, you are healed of your sickness!' Then he touched her, and immediately she could stand straight. How she praised God!"

Jesus has an amazing capacity to see broken people in crowds of others who seem quite normal. Coaches and their families can often do the same. When you are at your best, you not only work with the highly productive players but also with those struggling to keep up. The one who hangs around after practice is over may be as doubled over by pain in his or her soul as this woman in the synagogue. Jesus saw her and delivered healing with a simple word and a touch.

This is where the whole coaching family can be engaged. You can all watch for those on the fringes of the team. See those who don't quite fit in, who don't have rides home, whose families won't make it to senior night. Reach out, touch them, and help them to stand up straight. Your coaching family may be Jesus' healing hands for many.

Questions for Contemplation and Discussion:

1. Can you recall an instance when simply touching your spouse helped repair the tears in your relational fabric? Tell the story to each other.

2. Who are those around your coaching family who may have broken souls in need of a healing touch from you?

3. What sorts of touch are you both comfortable with in caring for others, and what is out of bounds?

Sweet Lips
Physical Touch
Day 4
Song of Songs 4:11

Can you recall the first kiss with your spouse? Okay, how about the most recent one? How sweet is that taste, how lovely the sensation? Can you imagine that the Bible describes such intimacy? It does and much more.

The Song of Songs is a book of intimate poetry and in chapter 4, verse 11 we read about all the writer experiences in kissing his bride.

"Your lips are sweet as nectar, my bride.

Honey and milk are under your tongue.

Your clothes are scented

Like the cedars of Lebanon."

This is not a polite peck on the cheek. This is not a quick smack on the way out the door. This is good old tonsil hockey, tongue wrestling, French kissing, making out at its best.

He says his lover's lips are sweet as nectar. I recall the sweetness of honeysuckle nectar in the summer and the taste of my first kiss with my sixteen year old girlfriend, now my wife. The intimate touch of kissing is as sweet as honey and as smooth as milk.

To smell the scent of her clothes as described here, they must be entwined in a loving embrace. She smells lovely and her essence fills his head with emotions that bond their hearts in a powerful love.

Most men are not poets, and most women are not fashion models, but when a husband and wife share the intimacy of a lingering kiss, their hearts are experiencing exactly what Solomon describes in this lovely scripture.

Whether you have been married four months, four years, or four decades, you need this sort of intimacy, this sort of touch to sustain your bond of love.

Here's the most pleasant challenge I will ever give you. Men, take a shower, shave, put on the cologne that drives her wild, get a breath mint and prepare yourself. Ladies, put on your most fetching outfit, spray on that knockout perfume, and get ready. Curl up on the couch together and let the making out begin. Enjoy the sweetness of each other's lips and the fragrant aroma of love. You can thank me later.

Questions for Contemplation and Discussion:

1. What do you recall about your first kiss as a couple?

2. Do your spouse's lips still taste like honey?

3. What is your favorite cologne or perfume your spouse wears?

4. Have you determined the day and time for the activities of the last paragraph? What are you waiting for?

My Lover's Embrace
Physical Touch
Day 5
Song of Songs 8:3

There is probably nowhere in society where hugging people is more widely accepted than in sporting culture. It's pretty common for teammates and even opponents to embrace before or after a contest. Today's focus is a totally different sort of embrace. For those of us who perceive love best through physical touch, nothing on the planet is better than the loving embrace of the one our soul loves. To hold that one close to our heart is the very height of intimate expression.

In Solomon's book of poetry, Song of Songs, he gives voice to his bride in verse 3 of chapter 8. In describing the intimacy she has with her husband she says,

"Your left arm would be under my head,

and your right arm would embrace me."

If you are thinking this reads like they are in bed together, you are right. The warm embrace of a husband and wife in their bed is the apex of intimacy. She finds joy, comfort, security, and enduring love as her husband gently holds her.

As the decades of marriage roll along, sometimes the thrill of intimacy and the allure of such loving embrace can easily fade. Even if the old man snores, if your bride no longer wears sexy lingerie, or the kids have worn you both out, make time to cuddle, to embrace, to share the intimacy of holding each other close. This is the stuff of mature love.

Coaching families are surrounded by pressures, urgency,

demanding people, and many other factors that challenge relationships. Use the physical touch of your lover's embrace to bond your hearts as you walk together through the fulfillment of your calling.

Questions for Contemplation and Discussion:

1. How often do you two cuddle together on the couch or in bed?

2. How important is such touch to each of you?

3. What are some of the emotions you experience when you are in the arms of your spouse?

Coaching: Our Family Business

Section 2 – Coaching Family Seasons
Preseason – Finding Each Other

- First Date
- Infatuation
- Could this be Love?
- Meet the Parents
- Engagement

Opening Day – Our Wedding Day

- Favored by God
- Friends of the Bride
- Here Comes the Bride
- I Do
- Honeymoon

Non-Conference – Newlyweds

- Who are We?
- Where are We Going?
- The Honeymoon is Over
- D.I.N.K.S.
- Family Planning or Glorious Accident?

Conference – Married with Children

- We're Pregnant
- It's a…. Baby
- How Do We Do This?
- We're _____'s Mom and Dad
- Launching Kids Into Life

Post-Season – Empty Nesters

- Peace and Quiet
- You're Moving Back Home?
- Spouse Rediscovery
- Grey Hair and Wrinkles
- Grandchildren are a Crown

First Date
Preseason – Finding Each Other
Day 1
Ruth 3:8-11

The sporting world is filled with aggressive and self-assured people. We see what we want and we go after it. However, when it comes to making the invitation to a first date, many of us are a bit more timid. How much flirting and how many awkward glances preceded the first date with your spouse? Who initiated the introduction? Imagine if you were to be as bold in your first meeting as Ruth was.

Ruth was not a coach, but her boldness reminds me of many female coaches I know. In the book that bears her name in chapter 3, verses 8 - 11 we read, "Around midnight Boaz suddenly woke up and turned over. He was surprised to find a woman lying at his feet! 'Who are you?' he asked. 'I am your servant Ruth,' she replied. 'Spread the corner of your covering over me, for you are my family redeemer.' 'The Lord bless you, my daughter!' Boaz exclaimed. 'You are showing even more family loyalty now than you did before, for you have not gone after a younger man, whether rich or poor. Now don't worry about a thing, my daughter. I will do what is necessary, for everyone in town knows you are a virtuous woman.'"

Boaz had heard of Ruth, but their first meeting is in the middle of the night as she curls up at his feet while he's sleeping. That's bold but also wise and humble.

Ruth demonstrated boldness by approaching Boaz, but her wisdom is seen in the timing, and her humility is seen in her words. She refers to herself as "your servant," and appeals for just a corner of Boaz' covering.

Boaz treats Ruth with appropriate respect and speaks to her in kind terms. He exclaims a blessing upon her, calls her "daughter" twice, praises her loyalty, and says that everyone in town knows her to be a virtuous woman.

This rather startling and awkward first meeting for a widowed young woman from another land and an older, wealthy man leads to wedding vows, children, grandchildren, and a family legacy that includes King David and Jesus of Nazareth.

Your first date was probably not just like that, but you can see where it has led. Where might you two be headed and who could be a part of your family legacy? Press on, together, and see where the Lord leads you.

Questions for Contemplation and Discussion:

1. Who initiated your first date? Where did you go and what did you do?

2. Were either of you as bold as Ruth?

3. How far into the future, into your family legacy, can you see today?

4. What do you hope that legacy will be?

Infatuation

Preseason – Finding Each Other
Day 2
Song of Songs 2:16

Have you noticed how selfish people are when infatuated with the objects of their affection? Professional coaches and players often seem to be overcome by the idea of winning a championship ring. Young lovers will say, "He's my boyfriend; he's the team captain." "She's my girlfriend. She's the Athletic Director. She's with me." Infatuation, whether with a dream or a person, is more than a little selfish in nature.

Solomon wrote about the nature of immature love, infatuation, in Song of Songs chapter 2, verse 16. There he poetically wrote,

"My lover is mine, and I am his.

He browses among the lilies."

The first part of this is pretty easy to grasp, but the latter part needs some explanation.

This young lady says, "My lover is mine, and I am his." The emphasis is upon his being hers. "That's my boyfriend, not yours." Secondarily, she will consent to being his, but primarily she says, "He's mine!" almost as if he is a possession.

Her lover is a wealthy farmer with cattle and vineyards. His browsing among the lilies refers to where he pastures his cattle. This dude is so hot his cows eat flowers! He has it going on. She's infatuated with him and everything he does is lovely.

This looks like when Ken and Barbie start dating. Everything about them seems to be perfect. There is not a flaw

61

to be found anywhere. This is the nature of infatuation. Its sight is often blurry, and its perception is usually dull. You may have experienced this.

Thankfully, relationships eventually outgrow this phase and either collapse or develop toward mature love. Coaching families must not get caught by infatuation, with goals, with people, or even with the person in the mirror. Let's nurture a mature love with our eyes wide open and our hearts full of wise perception.

Questions for Contemplation and Discussion:

1. What first attracted you to your spouse? Does he or she still possess those qualities?

2. What helped push your relationship past infatuation to a more mature sort of love?

3. What are some goals or dreams with which you have been infatuated in past years?

Could This Be Love?

Preseason – Finding Each Other
Day 3
Song of Songs 4:9

Can you recall the paralyzing analysis that accompanies young love? "Is this real love or just chemistry? Does she love me or just my image? Does he truly love me or just how I look in my uniform?" The Bible records these same emotions as experienced by young lovers.

Song of Songs chapter 4, verse 9 shares the emotional response of a young man to his beautiful, young love.

"You have captured my heart,

My treasure, my bride.

You hold it hostage with one glance of your eyes,

With a single jewel of our necklace."

This guy is smitten! His heart is captured. She is his treasure. His heart is held hostage. His emotions are overwhelmed by this woman.

His love for her, a good and proper emotion, is here described in less than healthy terms. To be captured is not usually good. To be held hostage is less than desirable. What's going on here?

Young love that's struggling to find its way is often like this. We wonder if the feelings we hold in our heart are mutually felt by the other. We fear rejection, but we can't stay away. We want so badly to love and to be loved, but we're not quite sure we can fully trust.

This is the point in a relationship that feels riskiest. It's where we express the captured nature of our hearts and ask if the one we love, loves us as well. It's scary.

As your love grows, and as your coaching family develops, make time for captivating glances into your spouse's eyes. Hold each other's hearts hostage with the beauty of loving intimacy. Rekindle the spark of love that flooded your mind with urgent questions so long ago.

Questions for Contemplation and Discussion:

1. Can you recall the anxiety of the early days in your relationship? How did you navigate those turbulent waters?

2. Are there things that have you analyzing your relationship today? How can you talk about it?

3. What will you do to rekindle the emotional spark of love and then fan it into flame?

Meet the Parents

How awkward was it the first time you met your spouse's parents? Some fathers want it to be difficult. Imagine if you lived in a culture where arranged marriages were standard practice. How clumsy would those first meetings be? How well would you handle the process seen in this couple's brief courtship from the Bible?

Genesis chapter 24, verses 63 - 67 chronicles the days Isaac and Rebekah meet, agree to be married, and meet Isaac's mother. "One evening as he was walking and meditating in the fields, he looked up and saw the camels coming. When Rebekah looked up and saw Isaac, she quickly dismounted from her camel. 'Who is that man walking through the fields to meet us?' she asked the servant. And he replied, 'It is my master.' So Rebekah covered her face with her veil. Then the servant told Isaac everything he had done. And Isaac brought Rebekah into his mother Sarah's tent, and she became his wife. He loved her deeply, and she was a special comfort to him after the death of his mother."

You're probably glad marriages are not still arranged this way. It seemed to work out okay for Isaac and Rebekah. Isaac's father sent a servant to find a wife among his network of friends and relatives. The servant brought one back, and there you have it; meet the parents, let's get married.

Husbands, can you recall your first awkward conversation with your father-in-law? Wives, can you recall the seemingly disapproving glare from your future mother-in-law? These experiences are pretty common, though less than ideal.

What's important to the process of building a family is the respect seen in both Isaac and Rebekah throughout the story. Each of them is respectful to the other, to their companions along the way, and to Isaac's mother.

One day you may be the parents in this awkward meeting, and you'll want a similar level of respect to be afforded you.

Questions for Contemplation and Discussion:

1. What are your memories of meeting your in-laws for the first time?

2. Have you thought about how you'll receive a young man who wants to marry your daughter?

3. How will you counsel your son related to speaking to his prospective father-in-law to ask if he may marry his daughter?

4. What are the expressions of respect you want from your adult children? Do they know how to do that?

We're Engaged!

Preseason – Finding Each Other

Day 5

Song of Songs 2:10

How did your marriage proposal transpire? Who popped the question? Was it a romantic affair, carefully choreographed, or more casual and matter of fact? Was it as poetic as King Solomon's proposal in Song of Songs?

Chapter 2, verse 10 records the bride's recollection of her husband's proposal.

"My lover said to me,

'Rise up, my darling!

Come away with me, my fair one!"

Solomon had more than two hundred wives, so I would imagine he said this more than a few times. Many of those would have been arranged marriages to align Israel with neighboring nations. Sadly, this proliferation of wives led to the demise of both Solomon and Israel.

This bride remembers fondly the loving expression of her lover in proposal. "Rise up, my darling." He's calling her to leave her mom's house and join him in making a life together. Does that sound familiar?

His next line is likely heard with both a measure of fear and a strong dose of affection. "Come away with me, my fair one." "Where are we going?" might be how you would respond. Calling her, "my fair one!" may overcome the fear with loving trust.

This sounds a little like a late night invitation to elope

and get married in a Las Vegas wedding chapel. Some fathers may prefer that to a $30,000 bill for an elaborate wedding and reception.

Whether yours was a church wedding with hundreds of guests or a simple ceremony with the Justice of the Peace, the proposal from the man to his bride to be is the same, "Rise up, my darling! Come away with me, my fair one!"

Husbands, call your bride, your fair one, to rise up and come away with you. Go anywhere you like, but be sure to sweep her off her feet. Do it today.

Questions for Contemplation and Discussion:

1. Which of you popped the question to propose marriage? How did it happen?

2. If you could do it over again, what would you do? Why not do that now?

3. When will you next say to your lover, "Rise up, my darling! Come away with me, my fair one"?

Favored By God

Opening Day – Our Wedding Day
Day 1
Proverbs 18:22

Somewhere along the way in a relationship's development, the man becomes aware of how greatly blessed he is to have this woman by his side. King Solomon was rich beyond measure, but he understood the nature of true wealth.

He wrote about real treasure in the book of Proverbs in chapter 18, verse 22, "The man who finds a wife finds a treasure, and he receives favor from the Lord." This man had more money than a thousand accountants could tabulate, but he sees his wife as a treasure. Even more than that, he says for a man to have found a wife is to have received favor from God.

A man begins to grasp how great a treasure his wife is on his wedding day. He looks down the aisle at this vision in white, she approaches him, she takes his arm, she takes his hand, she vows to love him, and she kisses her husband. His heart is profoundly enriched. A husband knows this treasure far surpasses monetary wealth, simply because money cannot love him in return.

The man who finds a wife has certainly received the Lord's favor. A wife's skills and gifts are usually different than those of her husband. She makes him better simply by being at his side. She complements her husband, and the couple are much more together than they ever were separately. This is the Lord's display of favor upon a man.

Whether your wedding day was a week ago, a decade

ago, or fifty years in the past, if you are a husband, you have found a treasure. You have certainly received favor from the Lord. Appreciate your bride accordingly.

Questions for Contemplation and Discussion:
1. Can you recall looking down the aisle at your bride as she approached the altar?

2. What do you remember about the first sight of your groom on your wedding day?

3. In what ways is your bride a treasure to your life? When did your husband most recently tell you of your worth?

4. In what ways has your wife been a demonstration of the Lord's favor in your life?

Friends of the Bride

Opening Day – Our Wedding Day
Day 2
Song of Songs 1:4b

Who were the bridesmaids and groomsmen at your wedding? How did they receive such places of honor? Can you recall their faces on your wedding day? If you were in coaching already, I'm guessing some guests may have arrived in team gear. Family and friends alike were gathered to celebrate and to consecrate your love.

Solomon writes in the voice of the young women of Jerusalem as they celebrate the love of the king and his bride. We read their expressions in Song of Songs chapter 1, the second half of verse 4.

"How happy we are for you, O king.

We praise your love even more than wine."

Like bridesmaids of today, these young women were alongside their friends to celebrate their love and witness their vows.

Two attitudes are notable in this group of friends.

1. They are happy for the king. They are not jealous of the bride, wishing they were marrying the king. Newlyweds need friends who are genuinely happy for the couple.

2. They praise their love even more than the wine at the reception. This group seems to really like wine, but they are even more taken by the love shared between the bride and groom. This makes for a better reception and better friendships after the wedding.

Beyond the wedding day, married couples need a good circle of wise and loving friends surrounding them. To walk through life with trusted friends eases the pain of difficult seasons and enhances the joys of coaching life.

Occasionally the families of a coaching staff get along well, and they carry each other's burdens, and celebrate life's victories together.

Let's be like these young women from Jerusalem. Let's be happy for our friends, family, and coaching colleagues as they marry. Let's praise their love and nurture it far beyond the wine soaked reception.

Questions for Contemplation and Discussion:

1. Can you name all the bridesmaids and groomsmen from your wedding? Where are they now?

2. Who in your circle of friends love you like these women from Jerusalem loved that bride and groom?

3. How do you both help carry burdens and celebrate with the other coaching families on your staff?

4. What would you like to do that you presently do not?

Here Comes the Bride
Opening Day – Our Wedding Day
Day 3
Song of Songs 6:3

An amazing transformation takes place in most wedding ceremonies, but it escapes the notice of many. The bride walks down the aisle toward her groom with one surname, and walks back out on his arm, suddenly bearing her husband's surname. She identifies so strongly with him that she even changes her name.

Song of Songs notes this same dynamic of identity shift in chapter 6, verse 3, as the bride speaks in these words,

"I am my lover's, and my lover is mine.

He browses among the lilies."

You may recall that earlier in chapter 2, verse 16 she said, "My lover is mine, and I am his. He browses among the lilies." The words of both statements are the same, only the order has changed.

We characterized her words in chapter 2 as being infatuation; madly in love, but just a little selfish. She started there with, "My lover is mine."

Here in chapter 6, she says, "I am my lover's." Now her first thought is identification with the one her soul loves. More than him being hers, she is now his. This is the central issue on a wedding day. These two now identify themselves, each with the other, even more than they assert their own individuality.

Wedding parties in our culture often get lost in the maze of invitations, guest lists, venues, dresses, tuxedos, limousines, caterers, reception favors, and an endless list of details. The most essential element of making the wedding a success is the bonding of two hearts in unified identity. The two become one flesh. Whether one spouse takes on the surname of the other or not, they enter the room as two individuals, and they depart as a unified husband and wife.

Coaching couples must find ways to affirm their collective identity even more than their public identity. The more celebrity and notoriety they are afforded, or with which they are accursed, this becomes an ever challenging task. It is of paramount importance that they each hold tightly to this expression, "I am my lover's."

Questions for Contemplation and Discussion:

1. Wife, when you married, did you take your husband's surname? Did you understand its significance at the time?

2. When do you remember the shift taking place in your relationship from, "My lover is mine," to "I am my lover's"?

3. How can you purposefully affirm your collective identity while the sporting culture tends to promote individualism?

I Do.

Opening Day – Our Wedding Day
Day 4
Mark 10:7-9

From the beginning of time men have left their parent's home, have joined with a wife, and they two have become one. In your life together as a coaching couple, how has your bond grown? How inseparable would you say you have become?

Mark records some of Jesus' words about marriage in his gospel in chapter 10, verses 7 - 9. There we read, "This explains why a man leaves his father and mother and is joined to his wife, and the two are united into one. Since they are no longer two but one, let no one split apart what God has joined together." He made this statement in answering some of his enemies who were trying to trap him with a question about divorce.

Jesus refused to play their pernicious games but explained the importance and permanence of wedding vows. His explanation rests on two primary points:

1. The husband and wife are no longer two individuals but are now one.

2. They are joined together by God. To split them apart would be foolish.

Our culture generally fails to recognize both of these essential values for marriage, and its fifty percent divorce rate attests to our foolishness.

When a bride and groom hold each other's hands, look into their lover's eyes, and speak their vows, God is listening in and joins their hearts together. He does this in fact, not in symbolism. We disregard this truth to our own peril.

As the bride and groom turn to face their guests and walk down the aisle together, they are no longer two, but one. They have each left father and mother, and they now belong to each other. Jesus said that no one should separate what God has joined together. Not a hateful family member, a foolish affair, a glamorous new coaching job, a difficult pregnancy, illness, disease, or injury; let nothing split apart this bond of loving commitment.

Questions for Contemplation and Discussion:

1. In your life together as a coaching couple, how has your bond grown?

2. How inseparable would you say you have become?

3. What are some factors that have threatened to separate your bond of love?

4. How do you experience God being the one who has joined you together?

Honeymoon
Opening Day – Our Wedding Day
Day 5
Song of Songs 7:10

Older couples say, "Honeymoons are wasted on new-lyweds." They have obviously forgotten the unbridled passion and unbounded love of their honeymoons. That night, the weekend, or week is important for launching the life-long process of building a bond of mature love.

Solomon's book of intimate poetry, Song of Songs, contains this third in a series of three statements by a young lady as she describes her loving commitment to her husband. In chapter 7, verse 10, we read about the consummation of their love;

"I am my lover's,

and he claims me as his own."

You will surely recall the earlier declarations made by this young woman as her love steadily grew. In chapter 2 she said, "My lover is mine, and I am his." In chapter 6 she flipped the order saying, "I am my lover's, and he is mine." There is a profound difference in her statement here in chapter 7. Suddenly there is no more mention of, "He is mine." She simply says, "I am my lover's." This love is selfless.

Also conspicuous by its absence is any mention of browsing among the lilies. All the external trappings she found so attractive are suddenly omitted from her speech. This love is intimate.

Whether it is discovered during the honeymoon, after

a couple of kids have arrived, or upon finding yourselves in an empty nest, every couple should experience this maturity of love, being selfless and fully identified in your spouse. This dimension of love sees the relationship, the bond between you, as its own reward.

Those older couples who talk about wasted honeymoons probably say that because they no longer need all those bells and whistles to love each other. Neither one look like they did on their wedding day, but it doesn't matter. What matters is their relationship. It serves as its own reward.

Questions for Contemplation and Discussion:
1. Where did you go for your honeymoon? How many days did it last?

2. What about your relationship is most rewarding to you?

3. How does your spouse communicate how greatly he or she values you?

Who are We?

Non-Conference – Newlyweds
Day 1
Philippians 2:12-13

After the rush and excitement of the wedding cere-mony, the reception, and the honeymoon comes the mundanity of real life, household chores, and the discovery of who you are now as a married couple. You are no longer two but now one soul. How do young couples unite their hearts to continue the development of their lives in Christ, now as husband and wife?

The Apostle Paul shares some ideas about this in his letter to the Philippians in chapter 2, verses 12 and 13. There we read, "Dear friends, you always followed my instructions when I was with you. And now that I am away, it is even more important. Work hard to show the results of your salvation, obeying God with deep reverence and fear. For God is working in you, giving you the desire and the power to do what pleases him." Here is talk about obedience and working hard, reverence and fear. This sounds more like doing the dishes in a small apartment than blissfully sitting by a Caribbean beach.

For newlywed coaching couples, the glamour of the honeymoon suite is quickly overshadowed by the more modest confines of a small apartment. The thrilling emotions of the wedding ceremony soon give way to the drudgery of long hours and stressful work.

All these factors lead us to pay close attention to the apostle's instructions:

1. Work hard to show the results of your salvation. Christ Jesus has worked in into you. You can now work it out in the world.

2. Obey God with reverence and fear. A healthy respect that knows God is in charge and we are not leads to obedience. So does a consciousness that there are serious consequences for disobeying God's way.

3. Undergirding both of these instructions is the comforting truth that God is working in us, both to desire the best and the power to do what pleases Him. Better than personal willpower, this is the power of God at work in us.

Okay, newlyweds, settle in for the long haul. Your life together will be full of thrills, pains, joys, and sorrows. There will also be long stretches of boring and normal. Get ready. Lean into the Apostle Paul's instructions, and you'll be well positioned for an enduring, loving, and growing relationship with the Lord Jesus and with each other.

Questions for Contemplation and Discussion:

1. When did you first sense the honeymoon was over and normal life was settling in?

2. What was plain old hard work for you in the first months and years of your marriage?

3. How have you sensed that God's power was at work in you to both desire and accomplish what pleases Him?

Where Are We Going?

Non-Conference – Newlyweds

Day 2

Proverbs 16:3

Coaching families seem to bounce around from job to job, but some of them surely have a plan for career and family development. How much of a plan for life did you have in your first days of marriage? How far into the future did you strain to see? What are the values and actions that insured your plans would succeed?

Proverbs chapter 16, verse 3 outlines some simple directions for setting a course into the future. It reads like this: "Commit your actions to the Lord, and your plans will succeed." That seems pretty simple, but there are a couple factors of great importance.

What does it look like for a coaching couple to commit their actions to the Lord? This would surely encompass all their actions. The way you go about your work. The way you manage your finances. The way you relate to family and friends. The way you interact with strangers. The way you deal with coaching colleagues, players, administrators, and officials. All your actions must be committed to the Lord.

The second factor is to have a plan. For a couple's "plans to succeed," it assumes they have a plan. It's wise to have a plan for family: planning for children, planning for a home, planning for savings, and many more factors in a family's life. It's wise to have a plan for your career(s): what to do, where to work, with whom to work, to pursue more education, or to be a full-time parent. It's good to have a plan. That's the only way you'll know if you're succeeding.

Here in your early days of life together, let me challenge you to sit together, dream, plan, and draw a best case scenario map of your future. Further, take some time to discuss how you will commit your actions, all of them, to the Lord. The proverb is clear, direct, and trustworthy: "Commit your actions to the Lord, and your plans will succeed."

Questions for Contemplation and Discussion:

1.   How much of a plan do you have for your life together?

2.   How have you committed your ways to the Lord? What have been the effects of doing that?

3.   Which of your plans have you seen succeed so far? Which ones are still in progress?

The Honeymoon is Over

Non-Conference – Newlyweds
Day 3
I Corinthians 13:4-7

Somewhere in the first days or weeks of marriage, you both became aware that the honeymoon is over. The grim realities of life accosted your wedded bliss, and conflict raised its ugly head. For coaching couples, this moment probably comes along more quickly than for others as they live in a world built on conflict. Many of them even like conflict.

The Apostle Paul wrote to his friends in Corinth, Greece and informed them of the nature of Christ Jesus' love. That was far different from Greek culture's idea of love. His eloquent words are in chapter 13 of his first letter to the Corinthians. We will consider verses 4 - 7. "Love is patient and kind. Love is not jealous or boastful or proud or rude. It does not demand its own way. It is not irritable, and it keeps no record of being wronged. It does not rejoice about injustice but rejoices whenever the truth wins out. Love never gives up, never loses faith, is always hopeful, and endures through every circumstance."

Most of us read this text and are immediately convicted that we don't measure up to this standard. Coaching life is seldom characterized by patience and kindness. There is a lot of jealousy, boasting, pride, and rudeness at hand. Many people are constantly demanding their own ways. Lots of people are irritable and keep long records of being wronged. For many in the coaching world, the lines surrounding justice and truth are pretty fuzzy. They like the last sentence a lot better than the ones above it.

Coaching couples who love Christ Jesus are called to be strongly countercultural. These values from I Corinthians 13 are our model for life together. If we simply float along with the general culture of the sporting world, it won't be long before we're terribly ill-equipped to deal with the conflicts that always accompany post-honeymoon marriage.

I challenge you to walk slowly through these characteristics of love, one by one, and consider how you can live them out as a couple. Take one a week or one a month. When you get to the end of the list, start over again.

Questions for Contemplation and Discussion:

1. What was the issue that caused your first post-honeymoon fight? If you can't remember, that's good.

2. Which of the characteristics of love in I Corinthians 13 are you doing best? Which ones are most challenging to you? How would you say your spouse is doing?

3. How might your loving in these ways have a direct effect upon the culture of your coaching staff and team?

D.I.N.K.S

Non-Conference – Newlyweds
Day 4
Proverbs 5:18-19

There is a season in a young marriage, before children make their magical and screaming arrival, that a couple revels in their love, intimacy, and the discovery of even more things to love in the other. Take your time. Some people have named this stage of marriage DINKs: Double Income No Kids.

Proverbs chapter 5 has some very direct language about avoiding immoral women, but buried inside those warnings is a strong encouragement in verses 18 and 19. There we read,

"Let your wife be a fountain of blessing for you.

Rejoice in the wife of your youth.

She is a loving deer, a graceful doe.

Let her breasts satisfy you always."

Here is a wonderful, poetic call for a husband and wife to enjoy every moment of intimacy they can and to find joy, beauty, and satisfaction in it. The husbands reading this are in hearty agreement.

Coaching couples in the DINK stage should take every opportunity they have to travel, adventure, stay up late and sleep in. They should go away for romantic weekends and be silly together. Soon enough things will change, and new responsibilities will squeeze these opportunities out.

If you're in the DINK stage of your marriage, let your spouse be a fountain of blessing for you. Rejoice in the spouse of your youth. Your love is beautiful and graceful. Let your intimate love satisfy you always.

Questions for Contemplation and Discussion:
1. How long was your marriage in the DINK stage?

2. What were your favorite things to do as DINKs that you could not do after kids arrived?

3. How has your life of intimacy and romance changed since your DINK days? Are you okay with that? What can be done to make your relationship more intimate?

Family Planning or Glorious Accidents

Non-Conference – Newlyweds

Day 5

Psalm 127:3

The prospect of bringing children into the world, into your home, and into your extended family can be both exciting and terrifying. Spending just an hour at the grocery store observing the wide range of parental styles and skills, the alternating giggles and fluids emanating from the babies, can give one pause when considering parenthood.

King Solomon, the author of Proverbs, Ecclesiastes, and Song of Songs, also penned at least one psalm. His psalm is a part of a collection called the Songs of Ascent. In Psalm 127, verse 3, he writes about the value of children.

"Children are a gift from the Lord;

They are a reward from him."

Whether carefully planned or not, anticipated for months or a complete surprise, Solomon says that children are a gift from the Lord.

No child is without worth, simply because each one is a gift from God. Solomon goes even further by stating that children are a reward from God. They are not inconveniences or encumbrances; they are rewards.

One of the blights upon the society of the USA is the way we have devalued children. The Bible is very clear about their infinite value, in this text and throughout the scripture. We would do well to embrace the view Solomon expresses in this psalm.

Remember these words of Solomon when you read the results of that pregnancy test, or when your bride says she has exciting news for you. "Children are a gift from the Lord. They are a reward from him."

Questions for Contemplation and Discussion:
1. Does a visit to the grocery store and observation of families with young children give you pause about having kids? What concerns you?

2. What is your approach to having children? Should you wait a while or jump right in? Why do you feel that way?

3. How can you demonstrate to others that you view children as a gift from the Lord and not an inconvenience or an encumbrance?

We're Pregnant!

Conference – Married with Children
Day 1
I Samuel 1:19-20

One day in the lives of coaching families is like no other. Whether well planned or a total surprise to you both, to discover that you're soon to be first time parents is a momentous occasion. Reactions to the news range from squeals of pure delight to panic attacks.

One particular pregnancy in the Bible was the fulfillment of many years of agonizing prayer and waiting. The story is found in I Samuel chapter 1, verses 19 and 20. "The entire family got up early the next morning and went to worship the Lord once more. Then they returned home to Ramah. When Elkanah slept with Hannah, the Lord remembered her plea, and in due time she gave birth to a son. She named him Samuel, for she said, 'I asked the Lord for him.'"

Hannah had waited many years for a child, but she could never become pregnant. In her frustration, she poured out her heart to the Lord in prayer. She trusted God with her dreams of motherhood.

Countless couples battle with infertility and feel the same frustrations and disappointments as Hannah. Many of them follow her example and take their appeals to the Lord of Creation. As helpful as fertility doctors are, prayer may be even more effective. Hannah went empty handed to her Lord, and He granted her urgent plea for a son.

Can you imagine her elation when she became pregnant

and her anticipation across the following nine months? Her years of waiting were each fully redeemed by the arrival of the infant, Samuel. Hannah fulfilled her vow and dedicated him to the Lord. Samuel became the man who bridged two eras in Israel's history. He became the last judge and the first prophet.

Whether your pregnancy is a joyous surprise or the culmination of years of prayerful waiting, to dedicate your children to the Lord, as Hannah did, is an important step in seeing them become all God has purposed for them.

Questions for Contemplation and Discussion:

1. What are your memories of the day you learned you would be parents?

2. Have you struggled with infertility? How have you dealt with the agony of waiting?

3. How could you dedicate your children to the Lord?

4. How many children would you like to have?

5. What do you suppose Jesus has purposed for your children?

It's a ...Baby!

Conference – Married with Children
Day 1
Luke 1:66

In the delivery room, as the little one makes his or her appearance, everything abruptly changes. Nine months of anticipation are suddenly fulfilled by a little person's screaming arrival. Mom and Dad, grandparents, all your family and friends rejoice with you. Many of them also begin to wonder, "What will this child turn out to be?"

One such birth is recorded in Luke's gospel in chapter 1, verse 66. There we read about how people reacted to the arrival of John the Baptist. "Everyone who heard about it reflected on these events and asked, "What will this child turn out to be?"

John's mother had long been unable to conceive, and his father disbelieved when an angel told him Elizabeth was pregnant. The angel made Zechariah mute until the baby arrived. These remarkable events led many to reflect upon what God may have planned for this child.

Just a generation ago there was much more mystery associated with the birth of a child. We almost never knew the gender of the baby until the birth. Ultrasounds were rare and expensive, usually reserved for potentially hazardous pregnancies. Fathers anxiously awaited the excited exclamations from the doctors and nurses, "It's a boy!" or "It's a girl!"

Much of that phase of mystery has been wiped away by technology, but the more profound mystery remains, "What will this child turn out to be?" The unfolding of this mystery takes a lifetime. We cannot know what lies before the child, but we can rejoice in this day, the arrival of the fruit of our loving union.

In the midst of the busyness, excitement, and noise of a baby's birth, let's also be contemplative and reflect upon who this little one will become.

Questions for Contemplation and Discussion:

1. What do you recall about the day your first-born arrived?

2. What were your concerns and fears in those first hours?

3. How accurate did your imaginations about the child's nature turn out to be?

4. What do you now expect your children will become?

How Do We Do This?

Conference – Married with Children

Day 3

Proverbs 22:6

Of all the jobs on the planet, the one for which we receive the least training is likely the most important: parenthood. Where do we sign up for "Parenting 101"? Who is the definitive authority for this crucial process? Is it Dr. Spock, Dr. Freud, Dr. Dobson? Who?

The Proverbs contain God's wisdom for daily life, and parenthood did not escape his notice. In chapter 22, verse 6 there is a simple and promising statement. "Direct your children onto the right path, and when they are older, they will not leave it."

"Well, that seems pretty simple. Put the little ones on the right path and turn loose." No, that's not really what that means. Directing them onto the right path is not a one-time event, rather it's a daily, life long process of communication and modeling.

The best parents I know take their roles very seriously and see each child as someone to love, correct, nurture, and direct throughout the child's lifetime. Children are not remote control toys. They are to be directed in a hands on fashion.

The promise in the statement is that, "when they are older, they will not leave it." That "when they get older" part is troubling. We're not sure when that time arrives. Rebellion, wandering, and sowing wild oats are sadly common seasons of many young lives. Most times though, the former wanderer returns to the path and follows his parents' direction faithfully and hopefully without too many scars.

Parenting for coaching families can be even more perilous than for others. Added pressures, periodic absences by one parent, frequent moves, and other factors complicate the process. The instruction and the promise remain. "Direct your children onto the right path, and when they are older, they will not leave it." Take time to discuss how you will give godly direction to your children, follow through daily, and one day you will launch them into the world and proudly watch them soar into God's purposes.

Questions for Contemplation and Discussion:
1. From whom have you learned the most about parenting?

2. How do you compare notes with other parents about how they give direction to their children?

3. What worries you about what you see in your kids? What could lead them to leave the right path?

4. When do you think your task of parenting is complete? Why?

We're _____'s Mom and Dad.

Conference – Married with Children
Day 4
Proverbs 23:24

At some point along the path of growth and development in your children, the modes of our identification change. Early on people say, "Oh, Jason is your boy." Before too long we hear people exclaiming, "Oh, you're Jason's parents! That kid can play." "Yeah, you're Suzie's mom and dad. Isn't she wonderful?" At first we're a little shocked at the loss of personal identity, but we are soon quite satisfied to be associated with our progeny.

The author of the Proverbs experienced this as we do, and he wrote about it in chapter 23, verse 24. There we read, "The father of godly children has cause for joy. What a pleasure to have children who are wise."

There are few moments in life that resonate with joy like seeing one's child excel. This is the stuff of ballgames, concerts, school plays, academic contests, and baptisms. Even more gratifying is to learn about your child's expression of faithfulness and godliness from others. To hear a teacher or coach praise one's child is an inexpressible blessing to the soul.

As we age and our children mature, it's especially gratifying to see them making wise decisions about their education, choosing a spouse, making career moves, and becoming parents themselves. It is a source of deep satisfaction and the realization of God's faithfulness in your parenting to watch your kids soar.

The day is coming, young mom and dad, when you will

no longer be just your own person. One day you will be widely recognized by your relationship with your son or daughter. This is a grand and glorious day, if it's because of their godly behavior and wise choices.

Questions for Contemplation and Discussion:

1. When did you first become identified as _____'s parents?

2. What was your first reaction? One of loss or beaming pride?

3. When do your kids give you cause for joy?

4. When do your children please you by demonstrating wisdom?

Launching Kids Into Life

Conference – Married with Children
Day 5
Proverbs 10:1

Some of the toughest days in a parent's life are the "firsts." The first day of stepping onto the school bus, the first date, the first time driving a car, the first day of college, and the first day of life on their own. Launching kids into life is alternately terrifying and richly rewarding. It largely depends upon the nature of the child.

King Solomon had many children, surely some who did very well and others not so much. He wrote wisely about this season of parenting in Proverbs chapter 10, verse 1. There it reads, "A wise child brings joy to a father; a foolish child brings grief to a mother." Though quite simple at first glance, there are some layers of wisdom to this proverb.

Fathers of wise children just about bust the buttons off their shirts as their chests swell with pride. I can recall watching my son play baseball at ten years of age, turning an unassisted triple play from second base. Someone who sounds a lot like me shouted, "Whose kid was that!?" That same father has had many more joy-filled moments as his son has displayed wisdom throughout his years.

Mothers, on the other hand, seem to feel the grief of their children's failure very deeply. When a son or daughter acts foolishly, their mother takes it very personally, like it's her own failure. Right or wrong, she still feels the grief.

As our children age, it feels like our ability to shape their character, influence their decisions, and direct their paths is greatly diminished. I find that feeling to be deceptive. We certainly have less power over the lives of our thirty-year-old children than we did when they were ten, but we still have authority. Even if it seems they aren't paying attention, our words of guidance and nurturing hearts have tremendous influence.

If you are about to launch your children into adulthood, get ready for some panicky phone calls, some tearful evenings, and some moments of overwhelming joy. They come with this season.

Questions for Contemplation and Discussion:
1. What do you recall about some of your child's firsts?
>   a. first day of kindergarten
>   b. first sports competition
>   c. first day of driving the car
>   d. first day of college

2. What does your child do wisely that brings you great joy?

3. What do the kids do that grieves your soul?

4. How can you still be influential with your children, if only from a distance?

Peace and Quiet

Post-Season – Empty Nesters
Day 1
Isaiah 14:7

It's an odd sound when the kids have left home and suddenly it's just you two again. The sound is quiet. No fights, no laughter, no crying, no crashes, just peace and quiet. It's a real adjustment to make.

Isaiah's book of prophecy includes a verse that describes this sound. It's in chapter 14, verse 7, "But finally the earth is at rest and quiet. Now it can sing again!" Empty nesters can hear this sound and feel this emotion.

The initial discomfort that comes from an empty nest is usually quickly overcome by a sense of rest, a settling in with the quiet, and a renewed heart that sings with peace.

Coaching moms and dads often explore their home and reimagine how to use the spaces formerly occupied by their kids. What once was their son's room is suddenly seen as a man cave for dad. Mom looks over their daughter's room and sees it as a perfect spot for her craft projects.

The first days of an empty nest are a great time for a getaway. Time to rest and be at peace allow your hearts to sing again. Leisure time with your spouse, formerly a rare occurrence, is suddenly the norm. Dinner out together now doesn't require seeing the kid's menu. Hey, this is pretty good.

When you become empty nesters, don't be in a hurry. Take some time to rest and to settle into the peace. Spend more time together and listen for your soul to sing again.

Questions for Contemplation and Discussion:

1. What do you recall of your first days as empty nesters?

2. If you're not there yet, what do you imagine these days will be like?

3. What could you two do together that you couldn't do with your kids in the house?

4. What kinds of songs has your soul begun singing again in this season of rest and quiet?

You're Moving Back Home?

Post-Season – Empty Nesters
Day 2
Luke 15:20

Occasionally parents get a call from an adult child announcing they're soon returning home to stay, *just for a while* they say. You hope. Recently launched, suddenly returned; what does this mean? "We've really missed you. When are you leaving?"

The gospel of Luke records the amazing story of one son's return home to his father. In chapter 15, verse 20 we read the climax of this lost son's return, "So he returned home to his father. And while he was still a long way off, his father saw him coming. Filled with love and compassion, he ran to his son, embraced him, and kissed him." This return home was the end of a painful season of rebellion, grief, and pain for both father and son.

Some of our kids boomerang back home due to failure. Some of them return because they simply lack direction in life. Others come home to get their feet back under them when a relationship has crashed, when they've graduated college and employment is delayed, or just because they're lonely.

Sadly, some of us have experiences like the father and son in Luke 15. Rebellion and an obstinate heart may have driven the child from your home. For mom and dad to patiently, prayerfully, and expectantly watch for the prodigal to return makes for a joyous homecoming.

Regardless of the reason for your child's return to the comfort and security of your home, welcome them, love them, and help them prepare to launch again. They're worth it.

Questions for Contemplation and Discussion:
1. When you were young, did you ever move back home after having left for college or your first job?

2. How would you respond if one of our kids called to say he or she was moving back home?

3. What would we do that could help our kids be renewed, refreshed, and ready to launch again?

Spouse Rediscovery

Post-Season – Empty Nesters
Day 3
Proverbs 31:28-30

One of the most wonderful facets of an empty nest is the rediscovery of one's spouse. "Hey, I remember you!" No longer carrying a baby or leading a child by the hand, your wife has suddenly reappeared as a lover to be pursued. This is a delightful time as you can get dinner at your favorite romantic restaurant without asking for a children's menu.

This stage in life is wonderfully described, from a husband's point of view, in Proverbs chapter 31, verses 28 - 30. There we read about a wife of noble character,

"Her children stand and bless her.
Her husband praises her:
'There are many virtuous and capable women,
but you surpass them all!'
Charm is deceptive, and beauty does not last;
but a woman who fears the Lord will be greatly praised."

In this season, a wife and mom is in position to live some of her most gratifying days. Now blessed with maturity and perspective, her children stand and recount the stories of how well their mother loved and provided for them. To hear one's children bless their mother is rich and powerful.

Notice how this husband praises his wife. He sees her as surpassing the entire world of virtuous and capable women. I hope you husbands can see the smile your bride would display if you were to speak of her this way. Further, I hope you make it a point to praise her like this.

The author offers his insight into the true value of empty-nest dwelling women. He knows the charm and beauty of youth are fleeting and even deceptive in nature. He knows the enduring faithfulness of a godly woman is both charming and beautiful in every season of life. Let's stand up and bless them, empty nest wives and mothers. They are to be greatly praised, pursued, and passionately loved.

Questions for Contemplation and Discussion:

1. When have your children said things to you that you now treasure?

2. How does your husband praise you? For what?

3. What about a young woman's charm is deceitful?

4. What is there about youthful beauty that quickly disappears?

5. How does it feel for your children and husband to praise you?

Gray Hair and Wrinkles
Post-Season – Empty Nesters
Day 4
Proverbs 16:31

Most of US American culture is obsessed with youth, and we spend billions of dollars to color our graying hair and spackle the wrinkles our faces have earned across the decades of living. Coaching families often have an advantage in this regard as they know the value of experience and recognize those who bear it by their silver hair, furrowed brows, and crow's feet.

Proverbs chapter 16, verse 31 speaks directly to the value of having earned those gray hairs. It reads, "Gray hair is a crown of glory; it is gained by living a godly life." Before you say it, I would agree that not everyone with gray hair has lived a godly life. Don't get ahead of me.

As coaches meet around the staff conference table, the ones with gray hair are given a little more attention, a little longer to tell stories, and a bit more respect because they wear that crown of glory. Everybody knows they have earned every single one of those gray hairs.

Watch a group of moms when they get together. There is a natural deference given to the silver-haired grandmothers. All those women recognize the wisdom and experience that has accompanied each strand of the grandmas' crowns of glory.

If you are the gray-haired one, wear that crown with distinction. The Bible says it's gained by having lived a godly life. I would infer that having led less than godly lives could have abbreviated some others' lifetimes before they earned their gray hair.

If you live and work among gray-haired colleagues and friends, show proper respect to them, defer to them, and listen to them. After all, they wear a crown of glory.

Questions for Contemplation and Discussion:

1. Why do you think our culture is so obsessed with youth?

2. As your hair has turned gray or turned loose, how has it changed how you see yourself?

3. Does your gray-haired crown feel glorious to you? Why or why not?

Grandchildren are a Crown
Post-Season – Empty Nesters
Day 5
Proverbs 17:6

An amazing thing happens in the hearts of grandparents the very moment they first hold their grandchild. A flood of unconditional love rushes through every cell of their bodies. and crowns gloriously appear on their heads. To kiss the soft cheek of one's grandchild is the crowning achievement of family life and the rich reward of faithfulness.

Proverbs chapter 17, verse 6 informs our hearts about the immeasurable value of being grandparents. There it says, "Grandchildren are the crowning glory of the aged; parents are the pride of their children." Proverbs is full of wisdom for all facets of life, and values for family relationships are no exception.

Crowns are worn by royalty. No one feels more like kings and queens than do grandparents. It is glorious to see these little ones grow and develop. To hear, "I love you, Papa," is the sweetest sound an old man can hear. For a grandmother to hold, rock, and caress her grandchild's hair is regal. As we age, many of our joys from earlier in life begin to fade away. They are, however, greatly surpassed by the crowning glory of our lives together: our grandbabies.

The perspective gained by age also allows us to observe the truth of the second half of the proverb, "Parents are the pride of their children." It is so very gratifying to watch one's sons and daughters parent their children well. To see how daughters look up at their father in wonder and admiration is an enduring joy. To see how children view their mother with great pride, untarnished respect, and unquestioning trust is invaluable. Parents are the pride of their children.

Whether you are in the active era of parenting or the aged era of being grandparents, I challenge you to fully embrace your role. Throw yourself into it. This season will be soon gone and its unique opportunities with it. Wear your crown of glory, and be the pride of your kids.

Questions for Contemplation and Discussion:

1. What do you recall of your grandparents that looked like they wore a crown of glory?

2. If you are a grandparent, what do you love most about your grandkids?

3. When do you perceive your children view you with great pride?

CPSIA information can be obtained
at www.ICGtesting.com
Printed in the USA
FFHW012323200819
54350615-60050FF